peak mathematics **3**

Alan Brighouse
David Godber
Peter Patilla

Nelson

Thomas Nelson and Sons Ltd
Nelson House   Mayfield Road
Walton-on-Thames   Surrey KT12 5PL

PO Box 18123   Nairobi   Kenya

116-D JTC Factory Building
Lorong 3   Geylang Square   Singapore 1438

Thomas Nelson Australia Pty Ltd
19-39 Jeffcott Street   West Melbourne   Victoria 3003

Nelson Canada Ltd
81 Curlew Drive   Don Mills   Ontario M3A 2R1

Thomas Nelson (Hong Kong) Ltd
Watson Estate   Block A   13 Floor
Watson Road   Causeway Bay   Hong Kong

Thomas Nelson (Nigeria) Ltd
8 Ilupeju Bypass   PMB 21303   Ikeja   Lagos

First published 1981

ISBN 0-17-421308-5

NCN 0647-13-0

Printed in Hong Kong

Editor   Anne Murray-Robertson

Art Direction   Sharon Lovett, Michael Kaufmann

Design   Sharon Lovett, Sylvia Tate, Julia Denny

Photography   Chris Ridgers, Dawson Strange, Janine Wiedel

Illustration   Lynne Cousins, Simon Stern, Paul Stickland

Photographic Props courtesy of Hestair Hope Ltd

Filmset in the Nelson Teaching Alphabet
by Mould Type Foundry Ltd
Preston   England

Programme reproduced by permission of TV Times (page 51)

Contents

Addition

> 3762 The number in red is worth 6 tens = 60.

Write the value of the number in red.

1.	2475	2.	3607	3.	4293
4.	5192	5.	6340	6.	1974
7.	9023	8.	4569	9.	7211
10.	8567	11.	3802	12.	2491

Add 10 to each of these:

13.	750	14.	890	15.	795
16.	401	17.	692	18.	990

Add 90 to each of these:

19.	1942	20.	6704	21.	257
22.	5470	23.	810	24.	4672

Add 700 to each of these:

25.	1640	26.	3507	27.	7084
28.	920	29.	2882	30.	4350

Add 3000 to each of these:

31.	1400	32.	3672	33.	496
34.	6002	35.	59	36.	2

Write these numbers in words.

1. 7243
2. 8041
3. 2904

4. 1011
5. 6319
6. 2007

7. 2096
8. 7151
9. 4305

Now do these:

10. Add five thousand six hundred and seventy, and two thousand and twenty-one.

11. Add two thousand nine hundred and four, and six thousand one hundred and forty-nine.

12. Add one hundred and seven, and one thousand and ninety-four.

13. Add four thousand and seven, and one thousand nine hundred and ninety-six.

14. Find the total of two thousand six hundred and eighty, and four hundred and seventy-one.

15. Find the sum of seven hundred and forty-three, and one thousand eight hundred and ninety.

16. Increase three thousand and sixteen by four thousand nine hundred and ninety-five.

17. Add three thousand and twenty-one, and two thousand five hundred and one.

18. Find the total of four hundred and ninety-two, and five thousand six hundred.

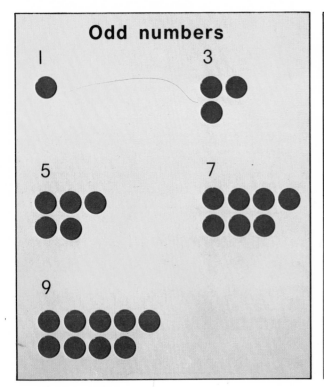

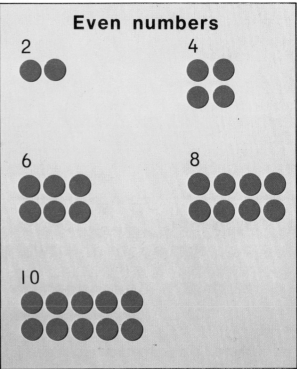

1. The odd numbers up to 10 are 1, 3, ☐, ☐, ☐

2. The even numbers up to 10 are 2, 4, ☐, ☐, ☐

Use the words **odd** or **even** to complete these sentences.

3. 12 is an (odd/even) number.
4. 17 is an (odd/even) number.
5. 20 is an (odd/even) number.

Write the odd numbers.

6. 9, 12, 18, 27, 11, 32, 14, 19, 43.

Write the even numbers.

7. 2, 31, 17, 54, 30, 63, 24, 36, 15.

This is an **even** machine.
It can only add numbers which give an even answer.

1. Which of these pairs of numbers can it add?

    (4, 3) (6, 8) (9, 1) (5, 2) (0, 9) (7, 11) (8, 3)

This is an **odd** machine.
It can only add numbers which give an odd answer.

2. Which of these pairs of numbers can it add?

    (5, 8) (7, 1) (9, 4) (0, 7) (5, 5) (3, 10) (6, 2)

Is your answer **odd** or **even** if you add:
3. odd + odd?
4. even + odd?
5. odd + even?
6. even + even?

Addition

1. 3762
    + 1498
    _____

    _____

2. 5097
    + 2704
    _____

    _____

3. 3292
    + 4875
    _____

    _____

4. 8277
    + 973
    _____

    _____

5. 4069
    1892
    +   28
    _____

    _____

6. 3873
    5278
    + 164
    _____

    _____

7. 4956
    1908
    + 2037
    _____

    _____

8.   947
    1858
    + 2216
    _____

    _____

9.   g
    465
    95
    + 280
    _____

    _____

10.   g
    318
    295
    + 185
    _____

    _____

11.   g
    274
    109
    + 85
    _____

    _____

12.   g
    394
    177
    + 298
    _____

    _____

13. m
    3·92
    +1·59
    _____

    _____

14. m
    2·43
    + 4·88
    _____

    _____

15. m
    4·61
    + 2·79
    _____

    _____

16. m
    2·74
    + 4·67
    _____

    _____

17. £
    0·69
    + 1·31
    _____

    _____

18. £
    3·87
    + 1·66
    _____

    _____

19. £
    4·06
    + 2·98
    _____

    _____

20. £
    1·73
    + 3·18
    _____

    _____

1. There are three classes at Stretton School.
   In Class 1 there are twenty-seven children,
   in Class 2 there are twenty-five children and
   in Class 3 there are thirty-three children.
   How many children attend Stretton School?

2. The headteacher had to order some coloured pencils.
   They are sold by the dozen; there are 12 in a dozen.
   He ordered 6 dozen red pencils, 5 dozen blue and
   10 dozen yellow.
   How many coloured pencils did the headteacher order
   altogether?

3. Monday is dinner money day.
   Class 1 brought £11·90, Class 2 brought £14·50 and
   Class 3 brought £12·30.
   How much dinner money was collected?

4. A van delivered 3 parcels of writing books to
   the school.
   One parcel held 480 books, and the other two parcels
   held 240 each.
   How many books were delivered?

Length

The length of the engine is 7·59 m.
The length of the tender is 5·84 m.

We find the total
length like this:

```
   m
 7·59
+ 5·84
_____

_____
```

The length of the tractor is 2·75 m.
The length of the trailer is 4·96 m.

We find the total
length like this:

```
   m
 2·75
+ 4·96
_____

_____
```

1. m	2. m	3. m	4. m
7·08	7·43	14·52	8·50
+ 4·97	+ 9·78	+ 6·64	+ 6·72

5. m	6. m	7. m	8. m
12·94	4·17	1·43	10·87
+ 7·67	+ 19·85	+ 12·77	+ 2·53

10

The height of the tunnel is 5·32 m.
The height of the train is 3·78 m.
We find the difference in height
like this:

```
      m
   5·32
 − 3·78
 ──────

 ──────
```

The height of the barn is 2·63 m.
The height of the tractor is 1·94 m.
We find the difference in height
like this:

```
      m
   2·63
 − 1·94
 ──────

 ──────
```

1.
```
      m
   5·18
 − 2·73
 ──────

 ──────
```

2.
```
      m
   7·72
 − 1·95
 ──────

 ──────
```

3.
```
      m
   6·04
 − 5·52
 ──────

 ──────
```

4.
```
      m
   2·84
 − 0·96
 ──────

 ──────
```

5.
```
      m
   3·50
 − 2·75
 ──────

 ──────
```

6.
```
      m
   8·14
 − 6·47
 ──────

 ──────
```

7.
```
      m
   7·52
 − 1·68
 ──────

 ──────
```

8.
```
      m
   9·73
 − 6·84
 ──────

 ──────
```

11

Side 1

Side 2

Side 4

Measure each side of this shape.
Record your answers like this:

cm

side 1

side 2

side 3

side 4

Find the total distance round the shape.

> The total distance round a shape
> is called the **perimeter**.

Find the perimeter of your exercise book.

Find the perimeter of your desk.

Find the perimeter of the teacher's table.

Find the perimeter of a room.

Side 3

Find the perimeter of these objects.

1.

2.

3.

4.

Subtraction

Subtract 10 from each of these numbers.

1. 442	2. 316	3. 975	4. 402	5. 384
6. 735	7. 892	8. 624	9. 854	10. 566

There is a quick way of subtracting 9 from a number.
Subtract 10, then add 1.

Subtract 9 from each of these numbers.

11. 315	12. 654	13. 724	14. 282	15. 596
16. 406	17. 633	18. 475	19. 842	20. 368
21. 501	22. 222	23. 745	24. 118	25. 390

1. 436
    − 108
    _____

2. 537
    − 241
    _____

3. 833
    − 475
    _____

4. 600
    − 449
    _____

5. 402
    − 138
    _____

6. 364
    − 190
    _____

7. 474
    − 197
    _____

8. 322
    − 85
    _____

9. 4846
    − 2657
    _____

10. 3349
    − 189
    _____

11. 2901
    − 1464
    _____

12. 5634
    − 2456
    _____

13. £
    8·42
    − 2·06
    _____

14. £
    7·40
    − 3·26
    _____

15. £
    6·03
    − 5·68
    _____

16. £
    4·00
    − 1·79
    _____

17. £
    3·84
    − 1·62
    _____

18. £
    9·22
    − 3·64
    _____

19. £
    6·10
    − 3·26
    _____

20. £
    5·25
    − 4·66
    _____

15

Subtraction

1. 4634
   − 1921
   _____

2. 5072
   − 831
   _____

3. 4186
   − 3504
   _____

4. 7342
   − 5422
   _____

5. 7380
   − 5421
   _____

6. 6395
   − 806
   _____

7. 4065
   − 2618
   _____

8. 3743
   − 815
   _____

9. 8217
   − 4630
   _____

10. 6384
    − 494
    _____

11. 5639
    − 3642
    _____

12. 6844
    − 5961
    _____

13. 6420
    − 673
    _____

14. 7163
    − 4284
    _____

15. 3621
    − 1744
    _____

16. 8365
    − 6877
    _____

17. 5304
    − 2647
    _____

18. 8400
    − 6523
    _____

19. 3604
    − 2815
    _____

20. 4200
    − 3673
    _____

21. 4325
    − 637
    _____

22. 7104
    − 2815
    _____

23. 7241
    − 5852
    _____

24. 5464
    − 597
    _____

1. 3046
   − 1752
   ─────

   ─────

2. 4018
   − 2631
   ─────

   ─────

3. 2040
   − 970
   ─────

   ─────

4. 3047
   − 1657
   ─────

   ─────

5. 8014
   − 6321
   ─────

   ─────

6. 3045
   − 2051
   ─────

   ─────

7. 6052
   − 4662
   ─────

   ─────

8. 8034
   − 6072
   ─────

   ─────

9. 5042
   − 4351
   ─────

   ─────

10. 7074
   − 988
   ─────

   ─────

11. 3064
   − 2175
   ─────

   ─────

12. 5060
   − 3480
   ─────

   ─────

13. 5042
   − 4363
   ─────

   ─────

14. 6070
   − 4484
   ─────

   ─────

15. 3062
   − 1775
   ─────

   ─────

16. 8025
   − 6736
   ─────

   ─────

17. 7032
   − 5146
   ─────

   ─────

18. 3072
   − 483
   ─────

   ─────

19. 6084
   − 4099
   ─────

   ─────

20. 3040
   − 1999
   ─────

   ─────

21. 8032
   − 3691
   ─────

   ─────

22. 6030
   − 2780
   ─────

   ─────

23. 3012
   − 734
   ─────

   ─────

24. 7058
   − 5139
   ─────

   ─────

This car park has four floors.
Each floor holds 240 cars.

The following number of cars were in the car park last Tuesday.

Ground floor 188
First floor   105
Second floor 183
Third floor   98

1. How many cars can the car park hold altogether?

Look at the number of cars that were in the car park last Tuesday.

2. How many more cars could be parked on the ground floor?

3. How many more cars could be parked on the second floor?

4. How many cars were in the car park altogether?

5. How many more cars could be fitted into the car park?

This table shows how many cars went out of the car park at lunch time.
No more cars came in.

Ground floor   89
First floor   48
Second floor   78
Third floor   19

6. How many cars were left on each floor?

7. How many cars were left in the car park altogether?

8. How many empty spaces were left in the car park?

Subtraction

1. 8000
    − 4624
    ─────

2. 5000
    − 1731
    ─────

3. 4000
    − 752
    ─────

4. 3000
    − 431
    ─────

5. 1004
    − 466
    ─────

6. 3002
    − 1463
    ─────

7. 4006
    − 2578
    ─────

8. 3001
    − 1644
    ─────

9. 6000
    − 3412
    ─────

10. 5005
     − 4216
     ─────

11. 5000
     − 3123
     ─────

12. 9000
     − 4724
     ─────

13. 8003
     − 5755
     ─────

14. 7003
     − 5344
     ─────

15. 8000
     − 988
     ─────

16. 6003
     − 4444
     ─────

17. 1000
     − 465
     ─────

18. 4006
     − 1987
     ─────

19. 3002
     − 844
     ─────

20. 3000
     − 1789
     ─────

21. 9002
     − 854
     ─────

22. 7000
     − 4683
     ─────

23. 3008
     − 2199
     ─────

24. 1004
     − 396
     ─────

1. 4032 — 465

2. 5000 — 647

3. 7402 — 2635

4. 7040 — 2551

5. 5021 — 3148

6. 2183 — 694

7. Subtract 253 from 6000.

8. What is the difference between 604 and 1741?

9. By how much is £9·63 greater than £8·92?

10. By how much is £4·63 less than £9·00?

11. What is 3124 minus 1756?

12. Take away 847 from 3042.

13. What is the difference between 7461 and 986?

14. From 3000 subtract 1462.

15. By how much is £2·73 less than £7·50?

16. Which number is 542 less than 3000?

17. What is 3144 minus 788?

18. By how much is 3622 more than 2756?

19. Take away 638 from 1549.

20. Subtract £1·81 from £7·64.

21. Which number is 201 less than 1160?

22. What is the difference between £6·03 and £1·67?

Shape

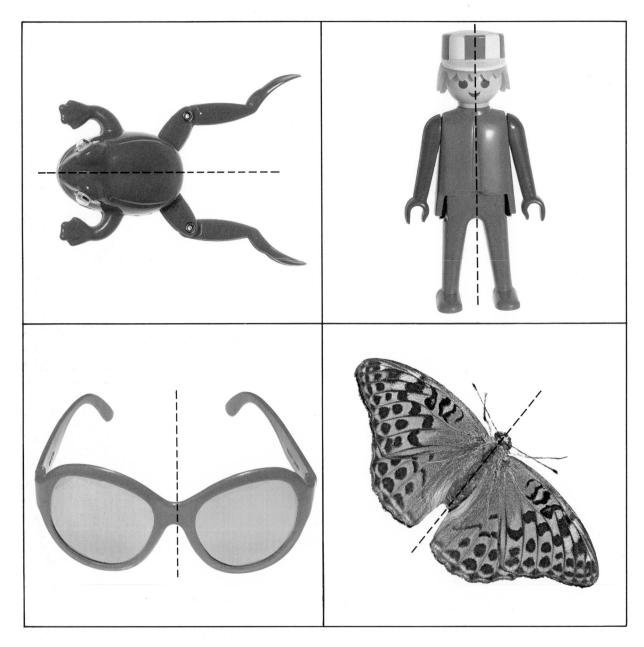

Place your mirror on each dotted line.
Tell your teacher what you notice.
The dotted line is a **line of symmetry**.

Plain paper, plane shapes

Fold the paper in half.
Draw a shape against the fold.
Cut out the shape.
Open the paper.
The fold is the line of symmetry.
Stick the shape in your book.

Remember: ≫ This means copy
into your book.

≫ This shape has a line of symmetry.

Do the same again, drawing a different shape.

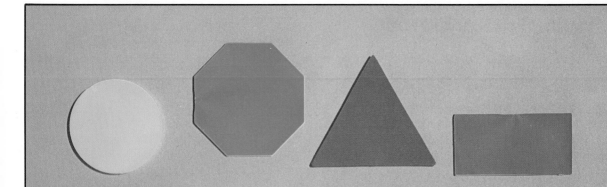

Find shapes that have lines of symmetry.
Draw round them.
Mark the lines of symmetry.
≫ These shapes have lines of symmetry.

Angles

Paper circle

Compasses are used to find directions.
They show North, South, East and West.
On the compass these are written N, S, E, W.

Fold your circle in half, then into quarters.
Label the folds like this:

Stick the circle in your book.
≫ This circle shows North,
  South, East and West.

1. If the farmer faces south, what will he be looking at?

2. If the farmer faces east, what will he be looking at?

3. If the farmer looks at the tree, in which direction will he be facing?

4. If the farmer looks at the tractor, in which direction will he be facing?

Plain paper

Fold the paper in half, then into quarters.
You have made a square corner.

A square corner is called a **right angle**.

Your right angle fits exactly between points on
the compass.

1. How many times does your right angle fit on
   the compass?

Which way do you face if you turn:

2. one right angle clockwise from N?
3. two right angles clockwise from N?
4. one right angle anti-clockwise from N?
5. three right angles anti-clockwise from S?
6. two right angles clockwise from E?
7. four right angles clockwise from W?

Set square

The **set square** also measures right angles.

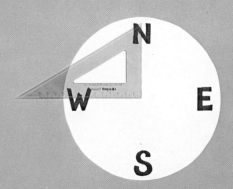

1. How many right angles can you find in the drawing of the boat? Use your set square to help you.

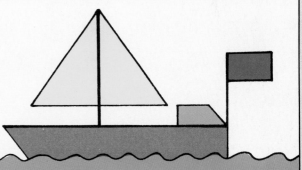

2. How many triangles, squares, circles and rectangles can you see?

3. How many right angles can you see?

Multiplication

Do these without using your table book.

1. $2 \times 4 = \square$
2. $5 \times \square = 30$
3. $8 \times 6 = \square$
4. $8 \times \square = 32$
5. $\square \times 4 = 28$
6. $4 \times \square = 12$
7. $3 \times \square = 15$
8. $9 \times 5 = \square$
9. $2 \times 10 = \square$
10. $\square \times 2 = 12$
11. $10 \times 4 = \square$
12. $6 \times \square = 30$
13. $7 \times \square = 21$
14. $0 \times 6 = \square$
15. $\square \times 10 = 30$
16. $5 \times 5 = \square$
17. $\square \times 6 = 24$
18. $10 \times 5 = \square$
19. $4 \times \square = 40$
20. $7 \times \square = 35$
21. $5 \times \square = 50$
22. $6 \times \square = 24$
23. $\square \times 10 = 80$
24. $\square \times 3 = 18$
25. $10 \times 10 = \square$
26. $\square \times 5 = 0$
27. $2 \times 5 = \square$

28.
$$\begin{array}{r} 27 \\ \times\ 3 \\ \hline \\ \hline \end{array}$$

29.
$$\begin{array}{r} 30 \\ \times\ 4 \\ \hline \\ \hline \end{array}$$

30.
$$\begin{array}{r} 28 \\ \times\ 6 \\ \hline \\ \hline \end{array}$$

31.
$$\begin{array}{r} 15 \\ \times\ 5 \\ \hline \\ \hline \end{array}$$

32.
$$\begin{array}{r} 33 \\ \times\ 5 \\ \hline \\ \hline \end{array}$$

33.
$$\begin{array}{r} 16 \\ \times\ 10 \\ \hline \\ \hline \end{array}$$

34.
$$\begin{array}{r} 49 \\ \times\ 4 \\ \hline \\ \hline \end{array}$$

35.
$$\begin{array}{r} 36 \\ \times\ 5 \\ \hline \\ \hline \end{array}$$

36.
$$\begin{array}{r} 58 \\ \times\ 2 \\ \hline \\ \hline \end{array}$$

37.
$$\begin{array}{r} 35 \\ \times\ 4 \\ \hline \\ \hline \end{array}$$

38.
$$\begin{array}{r} 22 \\ \times\ 10 \\ \hline \\ \hline \end{array}$$

39.
$$\begin{array}{r} 36 \\ \times\ 3 \\ \hline \\ \hline \end{array}$$

Build up tables for 7, 8 and 9 in your table book.
Show them to your teacher.

1. 15 × 7	2. 22 × 8	3. 30 × 9	4. 42 × 9

5. 74 × 7	6. 86 × 8	7. 63 × 8	8. 41 × 7

9. 39 × 9	10. 70 × 8	11. 54 × 7	12. 52 × 9

13. 63 × 7	14. 41 × 8	15. 70 × 7	16. 65 × 9

17. 84 × 9	18. 58 × 8	19. 69 × 7	20. 94 × 8

Do these without using your table book.

1. 164 × 2	2. 143 × 6	3. 124 × 8	4. 107 × 9
5. 186 × 4	6. 138 × 5	7. 96 × 10	8. 120 × 7

9.   208 × 4   10.   85 × 8   11.   119 × 8

12.   206 × 3   13.   179 × 5   14.   148 × 6

15.   Multiply 245 by 4.

16.   Which number is 3 times as great as 297?

17.   Double four hundred and eighty-six.

18.

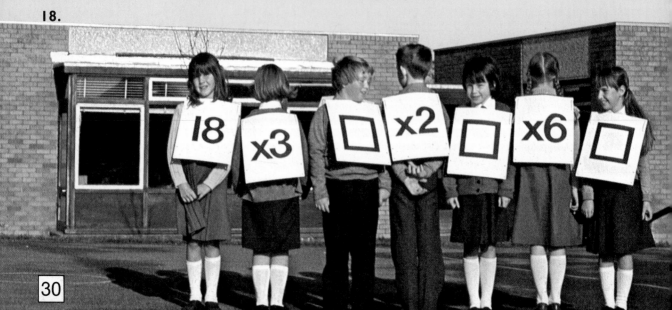

Tony goes to Highfield Infant School.
His sister Jane goes to Brockwell Junior School.

1. In the Infant School there are 115 children.
   In the Junior School there are 5 times as many.
   How many children go to the Junior School?

2. 75 children stay for dinner at Tony's school.
   In Jane's school 6 times as many stay.
   How many stay for dinner in Jane's school?

3. Tony collects stamps.
   He has 11 friends who also collect stamps.
   At the Junior School 10 times as many children
   collect stamps.
   How many stamp collectors go to the Junior School?

4. In Tony's school there are 68 boys.
   In Jane's school there are 4 times as many.
   How many boys go to the Junior School?

Capacity

Graduated cylinder, milk bottle, jam jar

You can divide a litre into **millilitres**.
I litre is the same as 1000 millilitres.
You can write it like this: 1 l = 1000 **ml**

≫ 1 litre = 1000 millilitres

1 l = 1000 ml

$\frac{1}{2}$ l = 500 ml

$\frac{1}{4}$ l = 250 ml

Fill a milk bottle with water.
Pour it into a graduated cylinder.

≫ The milk bottle holds ☐ ml.

You have found the **capacity** of the milk bottle.

Estimate the capacity of the jam jar.
Use the graduated cylinder to find its capacity.
Record your results like this:

Container	Estimate	Capacity
jam jar		

Choose 5 more containers smaller than the
graduated cylinder.
Estimate the capacity of each one.
Measure the capacity of each one.
Record the results on the list.

Write which container held most.
Write which container held least.

Write which container held nearest to $\frac{1}{2}$ l.

Write which container held nearest to $\frac{1}{4}$ l.

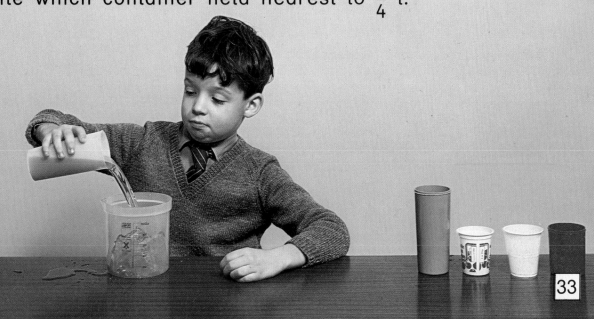

33

Fractions

Richard has a bar of chocolate.

Look at these pictures and complete the sentences.

1. ☐ is eaten.

   ☐ is left.

2. ☐ is eaten.   ☐ is left.

Jane has a different bar of chocolate.

3. ☐ is eaten.

   ☐ is left.

4. ☐ is eaten.

   ☐ is left.

34

Nicola has a bar of chocolate.

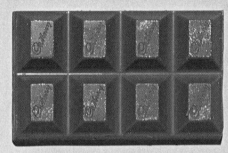

What fraction of the bar of chocolate is shown?
What fraction is missing?

1.

2.

3.

4.

5.

6.

7.

Add these:

8. $\frac{1}{2}$ and $\frac{1}{2}$

9. $\frac{3}{4}$ and $\frac{1}{4}$

10. $\frac{1}{4}$ and $\frac{1}{4}$

11. $\frac{1}{2}$ and $\frac{1}{4}$

12. $\frac{1}{4}$ and $\frac{1}{4}$ and $\frac{1}{4}$

35

This cake has been cut into 3 equal parts.

Each part is **one third** of the cake.

One third is written like this: $\frac{1}{3}$

Two thirds of the cake is left.

Two thirds is written like this: $\frac{2}{3}$

What fraction of each shape is coloured?

1.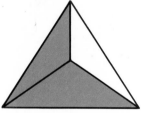

2.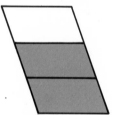

3.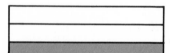

4.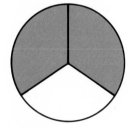

5.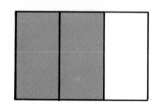

6.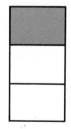

To find $\frac{1}{2}$ of a number divide by 2.

$\frac{1}{2}$ of 12 is 6.

Find $\frac{1}{2}$ of:

1. 4   2. 6   3. 14   4. 22   5. 8   6. 16   7. 10

To find $\frac{1}{3}$ of a number divide by 3.

$\frac{1}{3}$ of 15 is 5.

Find $\frac{1}{3}$ of:

8. 9   9. 18   10. 12   11. 27   12. 6   13. 21   14. 24

To find $\frac{1}{4}$ of a number divide by 4.

$\frac{1}{4}$ of 16 is 4.

Find $\frac{1}{4}$ of:

15. 8   16. 12   17. 20   18. 36   19. 24   20. 32   21. 28

Weight

Mrs. Foster is making a Dundee cake.
Here are some of the things she needs.

175 g currants	225 g plain flour
125 g dates	175 g butter
175 g raisins	125 g castor sugar
25 g cherries	3 large eggs

Mrs. Jones is making a fruit cake.
Here are some of the things she needs.

150 g plain flour	450 g mixed fruit
150 g self-raising flour	125 g cherries
225 g butter	5 eggs
250 g soft brown sugar	1 tablespoon black treacle

1. What is the total weight of the fruit in the Dundee cake?

2. What is the total weight of the fruit in the fruit cake?

3. How much more plain flour is there in the Dundee cake?

4. How much more butter is there in the fruit cake?

5. What is the total weight of flour in the fruit cake?

6. The cost of making the Dundee cake is £1·64.
    The cost of making the fruit cake is £2·58.
    How much more does the fruit cake cost?

7. What is the total cost of making both cakes?

8. When $\frac{1}{4}$ of the Dundee cake is eaten, what fraction is left?

9. If $\frac{1}{2}$ of the fruit cake was eaten one day, and $\frac{1}{4}$ the next day, what fraction was left?

Division

$$5 \times 4 = 20 \qquad 4 \times 5 = 20$$
$$6 \times 4 = 24 \qquad 4 \times 6 = 24$$
$$7 \times 4 = 28 \qquad 4 \times 7 = 28$$

$$24 \div 4 = 6$$
$$24 \div 6 = 4$$

Use your table book to help you to do these:

1. $12 \div 4 = \square$ 2. $20 \div 5 = \square$ 3. $60 \div 10 = \square$

    $12 \div 3 = \square$ $20 \div 4 = \square$ $60 \div 6 = \square$

4. $30 \div 6 = \square$ 5. $20 \div 10 = \square$ 6. $18 \div 6 = \square$

    $30 \div 5 = \square$ $20 \div 2 = \square$ $18 \div 3 = \square$

If we share 6 marbles equally between
2 children, they have 3 each.
We can write this in two ways: $6 \div 2 = 3$ or $2\overline{)6}$ with 3 above

Work these out and write them both ways.

7. Divide 18 sweets equally between 2 children.
8. Divide 24 chocolates equally among 3 children.
9. Divide 25 apples equally among 5 children.
10. Divide 30 marbles equally among 6 children.

Now do these:

11. $2\overline{)20}$ 12. $3\overline{)33}$ 13. $5\overline{)55}$ 14. $10\overline{)90}$

Base 10 apparatus

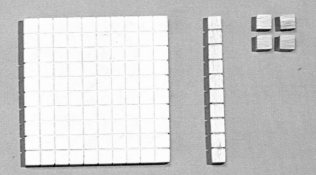

Put 114 on your desk.
Divide it into 3 equal groups.
Start by changing the hundred into tens.

1. Complete this: $3\overline{)114}$

Use the apparatus to help you to do these:

2. $3\overline{)117}$ 3. $4\overline{)160}$ 4. $5\overline{)135}$ 5. $2\overline{)144}$

6. $2\overline{)136}$ 7. $3\overline{)141}$ 8. $4\overline{)132}$ 9. $4\overline{)216}$

10. $5\overline{)150}$ 11. $6\overline{)102}$ 12. $3\overline{)123}$ 13. $4\overline{)204}$

Do these without apparatus.

14. $4\overline{)224}$ 15. $5\overline{)110}$ 16. $6\overline{)132}$ 17. $10\overline{)140}$

18. $2\overline{)158}$ 19. $3\overline{)222}$ 20. $4\overline{)572}$ 21. $6\overline{)372}$

Area

How many squares are there in each shape?

| Remember: 2 half squares make a whole square. |

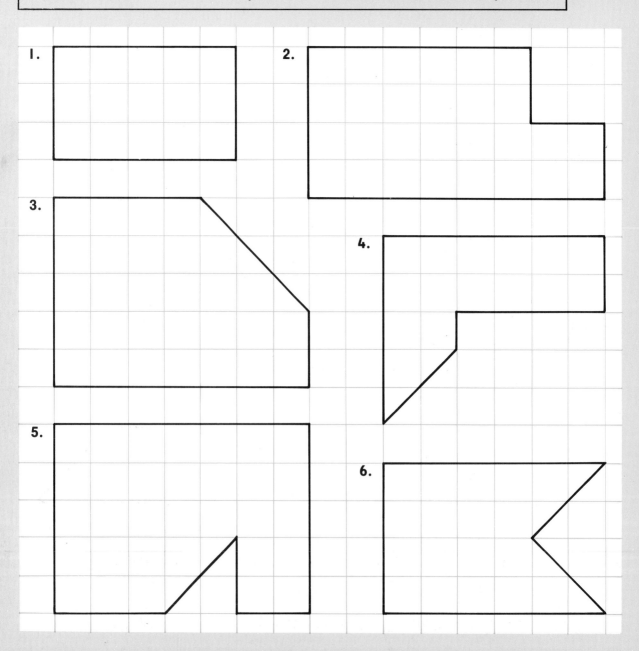

You have found the **area** of each shape.

Squared paper

1. Which of these shapes have the same area?

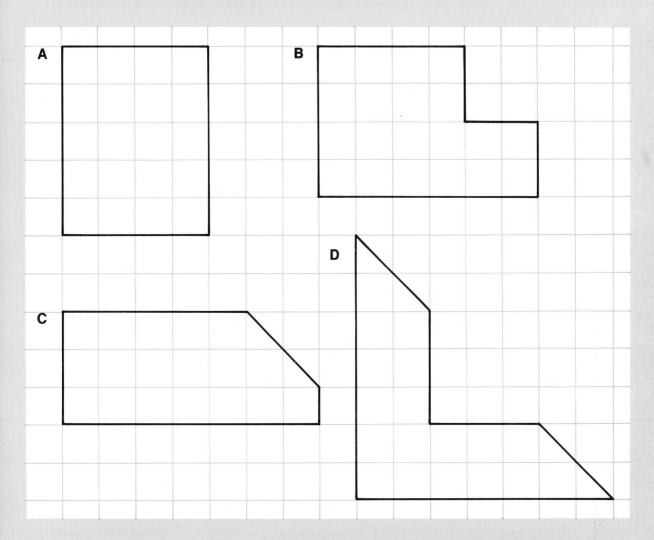

2. Draw four different shapes each with an area of 24 squares.

3. Draw four different shapes each with an area of $17\frac{1}{2}$ squares.

It is difficult to find the exact area of this shape.
There are whole squares and part squares.
Look at the part squares.

Some are greater than $\frac{1}{2}$ a square.

Some are less than $\frac{1}{2}$ a square.

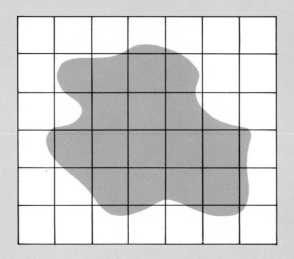

To find the approximate area:

part squares greater than $\frac{1}{2}$ a square count as
whole ones;

part squares less than $\frac{1}{2}$ a square do not count.

There are 8 whole squares.

There are 8 part squares greater than $\frac{1}{2}$ a square.

Count them as whole ones.

The approximate area is 16 squares.

Find the approximate area of these shapes.

Money

How much change will you get from £5 if you spend these amounts?

1. £1·50   2. £2·75   3. £0·38   4. £1·74   5. £3·72

6. £4·01   7. £2·83   8. £3·05   9. £0·75   10. £4·45

Now do these:

11. £1·64 + £2·09   12. £1·35 + £0·98   13. £2·74 + £3·39

14. £3·84 − £1·72   15. £2·73 − £1·89   16. £3·15 − £2·86

17.
$$
\begin{array}{r}
£ \\
1\cdot48 \\
\times \quad 4 \\
\hline
\\
\hline
\end{array}
$$

18.
$$
\begin{array}{r}
£ \\
1\cdot35 \\
\times \quad 6 \\
\hline
\\
\hline
\end{array}
$$

19.
$$
\begin{array}{r}
£ \\
0\cdot87 \\
\times \quad 10 \\
\hline
\\
\hline
\end{array}
$$

20.
$$
\begin{array}{r}
£ \\
1\cdot59 \\
\times \quad 6 \\
\hline
\\
\hline
\end{array}
$$

21.
$$
\begin{array}{r}
£ \\
1\cdot28 \\
\times \quad 5 \\
\hline
\\
\hline
\end{array}
$$

22.
$$
\begin{array}{r}
£ \\
1\cdot89 \\
\times \quad 3 \\
\hline
\\
\hline
\end{array}
$$

23.
$$
\begin{array}{r}
£ \\
0\cdot75 \\
\times \quad 10 \\
\hline
\\
\hline
\end{array}
$$

24.
$$
\begin{array}{r}
£ \\
1\cdot96 \\
\times \quad 5 \\
\hline
\\
\hline
\end{array}
$$

25. How much would you spend on a bat costing £2·75 and a ball costing £0·75?

26. What change do I get from £5 if I buy a cup costing 95p and a saucer costing 75p?

Blue paint   £1·75
White paint   £1·80
Yellow paint   £1·64
Green paint   £1·85

Peter's father is a painter.
He is painting Peter's house.

1. He needs 5 tins of blue paint.
   How much will they cost him?

2. He needs 6 tins of yellow paint.
   How much will they cost him?

3. He needs 3 tins of white paint.
   How much will they cost him?

4. He needs 4 tins of green paint.
   How much will they cost him?

5. How much will he spend on paint altogether?

Time

Both these clocks show 4 o'clock.
A short way of writing 4 o'clock is 4.00.
The first figure shows the hour.
The other figures show the minutes past the hour.

Both these clocks show 5 minutes past 4.
We write it as 4.05.

Write these times in the short way.

1. 10 minutes past 4
2. 20 minutes past 5
3. 30 minutes past 2
4. 40 minutes past 6
5. 50 minutes past 10
6. 6 o'clock
7. 5 minutes past 12
8. 35 minutes past 10
9. 55 minutes past 8
10. 15 minutes past 1

Clock stamp

Stamp 5 clock faces in your book.
Show these times on the clocks.

1. 8.40   2. 11.05   3. 9.55   4. 6.30   5. 7.25

Write the time which is 20 minutes later than:

6. 2.30   7. 3.10   8. 4.05   9. 11.35   10. 7.15
11. 8.40   12. 9.45   13. 6.50   14. 7.55   15. 12.55

Write the time which is 30 minutes earlier than:

16. 3.40   17. 11.55   18. 9.35   19. 7.50   20. 4.30
21. 2.15   22. 5.10   23. 8.05   24. 12.20   25. 1.20

26. The bus journey from Ambergate to Ripley takes
    25 minutes.
    Copy the times the buses leave Ambergate.
    Write underneath the times they arrive in Ripley.

Leave Ambergate	7.20 8.30 9.35 11.05 12.50
Arrive Ripley	

27. Make your own timetable for buses going back to
    Ambergate from Ripley.
    The journey would take just as long.

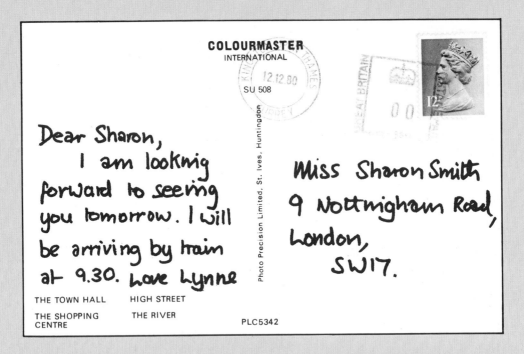

Sharon wondered if Lynne meant 9.30 in the morning or in the evening.

There is a way of showing the difference between times in the morning and evening.
   a.m. means morning
   p.m. means afternoon and evening.

So Lynne should have written 9.30 a.m. if she meant in the morning, and 9.30 p.m. if she meant in the evening.

Complete these, by writing a.m. or p.m. after each time.

1. School starts at 9.00.
2. I have my dinner at 12.45.
3. I have my tea at 4.30.
4. My father starts work in the morning at 7.30.
5. I go to bed at 8.45.

12 o'clock in the day is called **midday**.

12 o'clock at night is called **midnight**.

Write how many hours it is from:

1. 9 a.m. to 11 a.m.
2. 11 a.m. to 2 p.m.
3. 6.30 a.m. to 11.30 a.m.
4. 7.25 p.m. to 10.25 p.m.
5. 10.15 a.m. to 2.15 p.m.
6. 8.30 a.m. to 12.30 p.m.
7. 6 p.m. to midnight.
8. Midday to 7 p.m.

DEC 17 **WEDNESDAY**

5.15
The Brady Bunch
The Subject was Noses
The most popular boy at school breaks a date with Marcia, just because she has a swollen nose.

News at 5.45

6.0 Thames News
Andrew Gardner and Rita Carter with the Thames news, sport and weather.

6.25 Help!
Teenagers Zadoc Nava and Sarah Kogan with more ideas for young people.

6.35 Crossroads
7.0 This is Your Life
EAMONN ANDREWS

7.30 Coronation Street
How will Emily Swain deal with the gossip that surrounds her? Hilda Ogden becomes a real-life boss—for the first time in her life.

8.0 Secombe with Music
9.0 Love in a Cold Climate
BY NANCY MITFORD, ADAPTED BY SIMON RAVEN
JUDI DENCH

10.0 News at Ten
10.30 In Troubled Waters
Cutting pollution means tougher controls on shipping—a move long resisted by British governments, which have stressed the importance of maintaining the "freedom of the sea".

12.25 Close

---

9. Work out how long each programme lasts.

10. Which programme is the longest?

11. Which programme is the shortest?

12. How much time did "News" take altogether?

Graphs

Squared paper

The children in John's class are good at swimming.
They win swimming certificates.
The easiest to win is Grade 1.
The hardest to win is Grade 6.

This table shows how many certificates they have won.

Certificate	Grade 1	Grade 2	Grade 3	Grade 4	Grade 5	Grade 6
Number of children	24	20	16	12	8	2

John wanted to draw a graph of this information.
He cut a piece of squared paper 10 squares wide and
15 squares high to draw it on.
Get a piece of squared paper the same size and draw
the graph for him.
The vertical axis needs to go up in 2s.
Don't forget the labels.

This graph shows the number of children who went to John's swimming baths one week during the holidays.

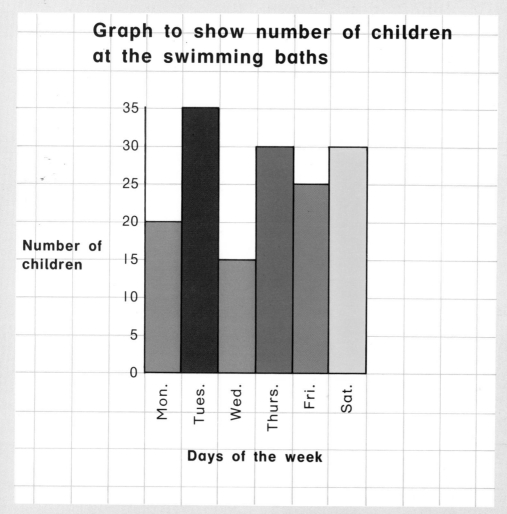

1. How many children were at the baths each day?
2. Which day had the fewest children swimming?
3. Which day had most children swimming?
4. How many children altogether were at the baths in the first 3 days?
5. How many children altogether went to the baths that week?

John likes reading as well as swimming.
He goes to the library every week.
One week he asked the lady at the library to keep a
count of how many children visited the library each day.
This graph shows the information he wanted.

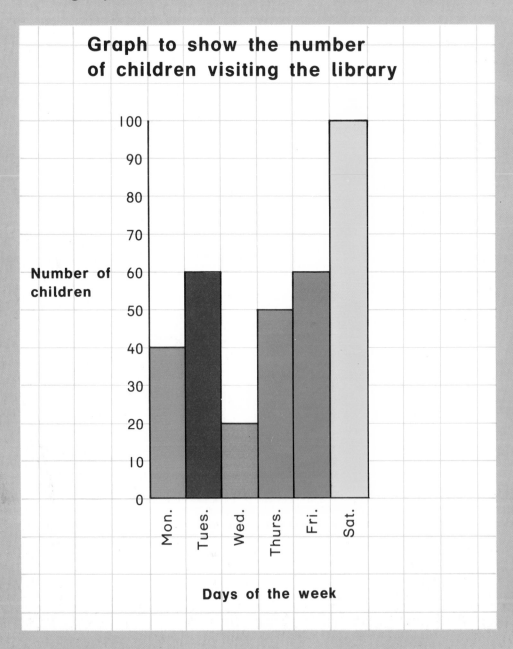

**Graph to show the number
of children visiting the library**

Number of
children

Days of the week

Help John to find this information.

1. On which day did most children visit the library?

2. On which day did the fewest children visit the library?

3. Which two days had the same number of children?

4. How many more children went to the library on Saturday than on Wednesday?

5. Which day had half as many children visit the library as Saturday?

6. Which day had twice as many children visit the library as Wednesday?

7. How many children altogether visited the library during the week?

8. On which day was the library not open?

9. On which day do you think the library closed at dinner time?

10. Why do you think so many children called at the library on Saturday?

Investigations

Card, scissors

Tessellating tiles can be made from squares.

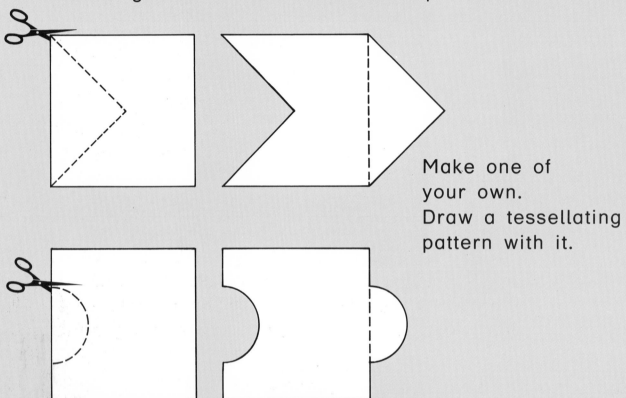

Make one of
your own.
Draw a tessellating
pattern with it.

Here is another way of making a tessellating tile.

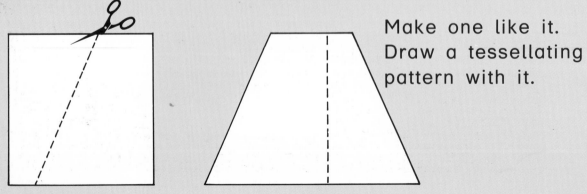

Make one like it.
Draw a tessellating
pattern with it.

Here is a more difficult tessellating tile.

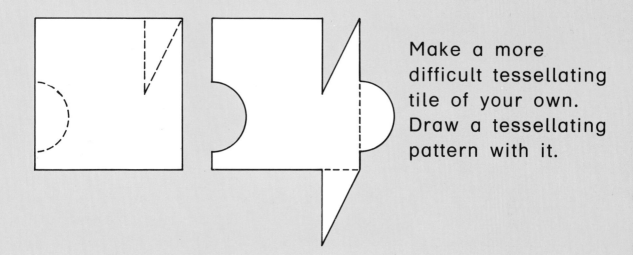

Make a more difficult tessellating tile of your own. Draw a tessellating pattern with it.

Can you make a tessellating tile from a triangle? If you can, make one and draw a tessellating pattern.

Investigations

This is a magic square.
Each row adds up to 15.
Each column adds up to 15.
Each diagonal adds up to 15.

4	3	8
9	5	1
2	7	6

It is thought that magic
squares were discovered in
2200 B.C. by Emperor Yu.
They were called the Lo-shu.

Dot patterns were used
instead of numbers.

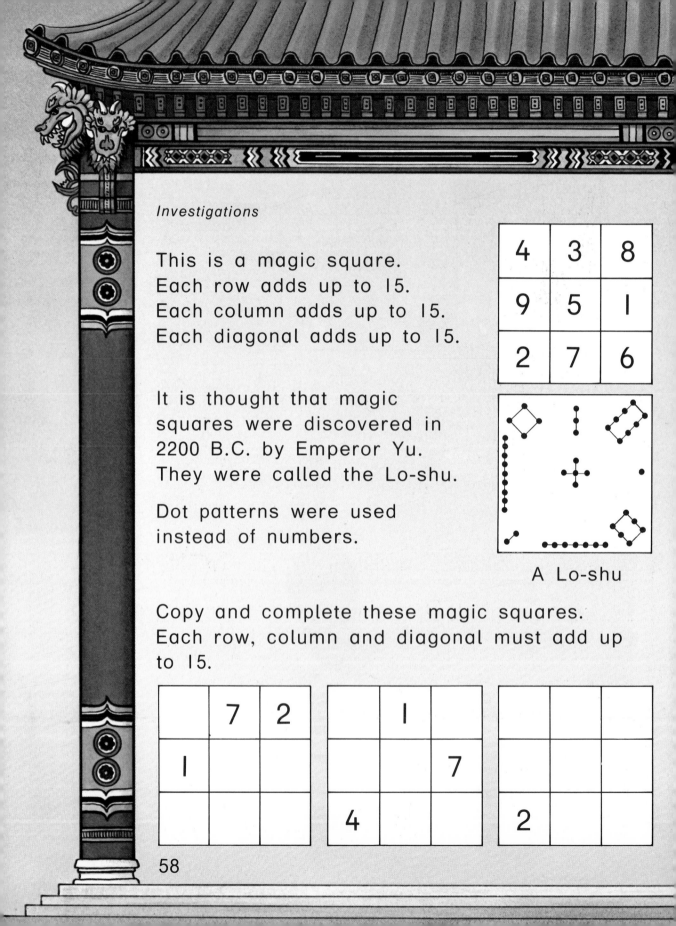

A Lo-shu

Copy and complete these magic squares.
Each row, column and diagonal must add up
to 15.

	7	2
1		

	1	
		7
	4	

	2	

58

Add 3 to each number in this magic square.
Is it still a magic square?

Multiply each number in the magic square by 5.
Is it still a magic square?

4	3	8
9	5	1
2	7	6

What has been done to the numbers in the magic square at the top of the page to give these:

9	8	13
14	10	6
7	12	11

2	$1\frac{1}{2}$	4
$4\frac{1}{2}$	$2\frac{1}{2}$	$\frac{1}{2}$
1	$3\frac{1}{2}$	3

9	7	17
19	11	3
5	15	13

7	5	15
17	9	1
3	13	11

Copy and complete this magic square.
Each row, column and diagonal must add up to 34.

1		14	4
	10		
13	3		16

Equaliser balance

How many washers are there on each number?

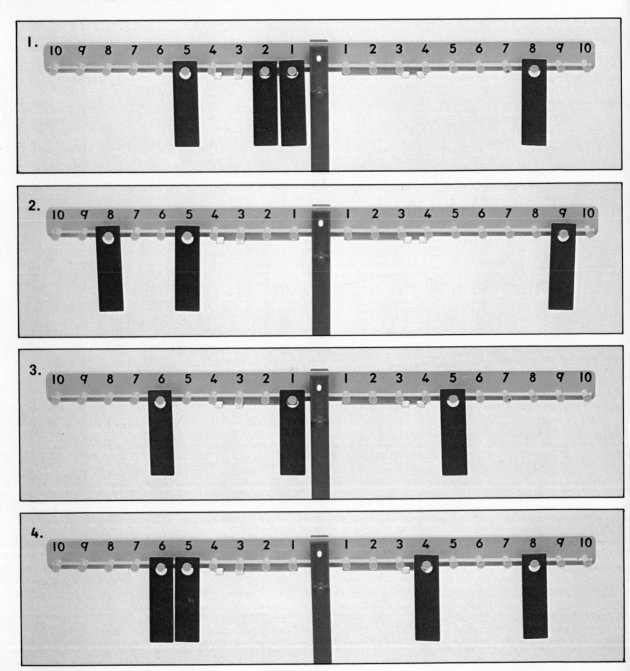

Squared paper

The mouse wants to reach the cheese.
It can only go along the paths.

Which is the shortest route to the cheese?
Is there more than one short route?

How many short routes are there?
Record the routes on squared paper.

Problem Page

John and Cathryn visited the fair.
They were given £2·50 each.

1. John had five rides on the dodgems at 25p a ride.
How much did it cost him?

2. Cathryn had three rides on the big dipper at
35p a ride. How much did it cost her?

3. The ghost train holds 52 people. On five rides it
was full. How many people did it carry altogether on
these five rides?

4. The big wheel holds 42 people but only $\frac{1}{3}$ of the
seats were full. How many people rode
on the big wheel?

5. John bought three bars of chocolate costing
14p each, and two cans of drink costing 22p each.
How much did he spend?

6. Cathryn treated herself to a candy floss, a toffee apple and an ice-cream.
   How much did it cost her?

7. How much did each child spend at the fair?

8. The children caught a bus to the fair and another one home. The single fare was 14p.
   How much did each child have left when they reached home?

Addition – more practice

1. 3621
    + 472
    _____

2. 4009
    + 3178
    _____

3. 2963
    + 1874
    _____

4. 2862
    + 989
    _____

5. 3725
    + 2996
    _____

6. 3718
    + 2382
    _____

7. 4079
    + 3984
    _____

8.   625
    + 2867
    _____

9. 1689
    + 2536
    _____

10. 2824
    + 1748
    _____

11. 5991
    +   9
    _____

12. 4920
    + 3089
    _____

13. 1063
    + 297
    _____

14. 978
    + 1364
    _____

15. 2704
    +   69
    _____

16. 299
    + 876
    _____

17. 2876
    + 1437
    _____

18. 299
    + 3863
    _____

19. 4731
    + 2673
    _____

20. 4152
    + 1869
    _____

21. 1721
    3699
    + 483
    _____

22. 2013
    488
    + 6979
    _____

23. 2116
    3729
    + 2096
    _____

24. 3114
    2725
    + 2271
    _____

Subtraction – more practice

1. 3821
   − 1701
   _____

2. 3196
   − 1845
   _____

3. 4026
   − 1308
   _____

4. 2947
   − 973
   _____

5. 3112
   − 2846
   _____

6. 1073
   − 849
   _____

7. 6814
   − 2918
   _____

8. 7332
   − 1046
   _____

9. 3060
   − 1728
   _____

10. 5264
    − 3973
    _____

11. 8400
    − 1620
    _____

12. 3148
    − 2909
    _____

13. 6008
    − 249
    _____

14. 1716
    − 1438
    _____

15. 6001
    − 5999
    _____

16. 4618
    − 2989
    _____

17. 3002
    − 1483
    _____

18. 4173
    − 2885
    _____

19. 4000
    − 3810
    _____

20. 8000
    − 6042
    _____

21. 7392
    − 4818
    _____

22. 1006
    − 869
    _____

23. 6831
    − 3482
    _____

24. 8925
    − 3926
    _____

Multiplication – more practice

1.
$$\begin{array}{r} 413 \\ \times\ \ 2 \\ \hline \\ \hline \end{array}$$

2.
$$\begin{array}{r} 208 \\ \times\ \ 4 \\ \hline \\ \hline \end{array}$$

3.
$$\begin{array}{r} 186 \\ \times\ \ 5 \\ \hline \\ \hline \end{array}$$

4.
$$\begin{array}{r} 314 \\ \times\ \ 3 \\ \hline \\ \hline \end{array}$$

5.
$$\begin{array}{r} 113 \\ \times\ \ 7 \\ \hline \\ \hline \end{array}$$

6.
$$\begin{array}{r} 106 \\ \times\ \ 9 \\ \hline \\ \hline \end{array}$$

7.
$$\begin{array}{r} 77 \\ \times\ 10 \\ \hline \\ \hline \end{array}$$

8.
$$\begin{array}{r} 149 \\ \times\ \ 6 \\ \hline \\ \hline \end{array}$$

9.
$$\begin{array}{r} 89 \\ \times\ \ 8 \\ \hline \\ \hline \end{array}$$

10.
$$\begin{array}{r} 137 \\ \times\ \ 6 \\ \hline \\ \hline \end{array}$$

11.
$$\begin{array}{r} 249 \\ \times\ \ 4 \\ \hline \\ \hline \end{array}$$

12.
$$\begin{array}{r} 65 \\ \times\ 10 \\ \hline \\ \hline \end{array}$$

13.
$$\begin{array}{r} 326 \\ \times\ \ 3 \\ \hline \\ \hline \end{array}$$

14.
$$\begin{array}{r} 226 \\ \times\ \ 4 \\ \hline \\ \hline \end{array}$$

15.
$$\begin{array}{r} 129 \\ \times\ \ 7 \\ \hline \\ \hline \end{array}$$

16.
$$\begin{array}{r} 123 \\ \times\ \ 8 \\ \hline \\ \hline \end{array}$$

17.
$$\begin{array}{r} 109 \\ \times\ \ 9 \\ \hline \\ \hline \end{array}$$

18.
$$\begin{array}{r} 169 \\ \times\ \ 5 \\ \hline \\ \hline \end{array}$$

19.
$$\begin{array}{r} 487 \\ \times\ \ 2 \\ \hline \\ \hline \end{array}$$

20.
$$\begin{array}{r} 159 \\ \times\ \ 6 \\ \hline \\ \hline \end{array}$$

21.
$$\begin{array}{r} 228 \\ \times\ \ 3 \\ \hline \\ \hline \end{array}$$

22.
$$\begin{array}{r} 107 \\ \times\ \ 7 \\ \hline \\ \hline \end{array}$$

23.
$$\begin{array}{r} 72 \\ \times\ \ 8 \\ \hline \\ \hline \end{array}$$

24.
$$\begin{array}{r} 95 \\ \times\ 10 \\ \hline \\ \hline \end{array}$$

Division – more practice

1. $4 \overline{)484}$ 2. $3 \overline{)573}$ 3. $5 \overline{)365}$ 4. $7 \overline{)847}$

5. $8 \overline{)472}$ 6. $6 \overline{)876}$ 7. $5 \overline{)700}$ 8. $9 \overline{)738}$

9. $10 \overline{)830}$ 10. $2 \overline{)992}$ 11. $7 \overline{)973}$ 12. $8 \overline{)936}$

13. $6 \overline{)444}$ 14. $4 \overline{)960}$ 15. $9 \overline{)396}$ 16. $7 \overline{)420}$

17. Divide 505 by 5.

18. Divide 800 by 10.

19. How many 6's in 912?

20. How many 7's in 217?

21. Divide nine hundred and forty-five by 9.

22. Divide eight hundred and twenty-four by 4.

23. Divide three hundred and seventy-eight by 3.

24. Divide five hundred and seventy-six by 6.

25. $843 \div 3$ 26. $486 \div 6$ 27. $705 \div 5$

28. $294 \div 7$ 29. $744 \div 8$ 30. $630 \div 10$

Money – more practice

1. £
   3·88
   + 1·09
   ———
   ———

2. £
   5·17
   + 2·93
   ———
   ———

3. £
   3·59
   + 0·93
   ———
   ———

4. £
   6·05
   + 2·97
   ———
   ———

5. £
   3·72
   − 1·50
   ———
   ———

6. £
   5·06
   − 3·84
   ———
   ———

7. £
   6·21
   − 2·96
   ———
   ———

8. £
   8·06
   − 2·59
   ———
   ———

9. £
   1·07
   ×   6
   ———
   ———

10. £
    0·96
    ×   5
    ———
    ———

11. £
    1·17
    ×   8
    ———
    ———

12. £
    0·87
    ×   9
    ———
    ———

13. £
    1·36
    2·96
    + 0·38
    ———
    ———

14. £
    4·09
    2·74
    + 3·26
    ———
    ———

15. £
    6·93
    2·97
    + 1·85
    ———
    ———

16. £
    2·00
    6·94
    + 3·87
    ———
    ———

17. Find the total of £1·39, £2·74 and £0·37.

18. Find the difference between £7·21 and £3·84.

19. Add together £2·03, £4·62, and £1·60.

Measurement – more practice

1. m
$$1 \cdot 37$$
$$+ 2 \cdot 43$$
_____

2. m
$$0 \cdot 78$$
$$+ 2 \cdot 49$$
_____

3. m
$$3 \cdot 39$$
$$+ 1 \cdot 58$$
_____

4. m
$$0 \cdot 54$$
$$+ 3 \cdot 96$$
_____

5. m
$$4 \cdot 06$$
$$2 \cdot 81$$
$$+ 0 \cdot 16$$
_____

6. m
$$2 \cdot 88$$
$$1 \cdot 64$$
$$+ 2 \cdot 35$$
_____

7. m
$$3 \cdot 33$$
$$1 \cdot 49$$
$$+ 0 \cdot 62$$
_____

8. m
$$2 \cdot 08$$
$$1 \cdot 72$$
$$+ 3 \cdot 44$$
_____

9. m
$$4 \cdot 06$$
$$- 3 \cdot 88$$
_____

10. m
$$6 \cdot 21$$
$$- 2 \cdot 87$$
_____

11. m
$$3 \cdot 94$$
$$- 1 \cdot 79$$
_____

12. m
$$6 \cdot 20$$
$$- 2 \cdot 83$$
_____

13. g
$$270$$
$$+ 150$$
_____

14. g
$$395$$
$$+ 240$$
_____

15. g
$$350$$
$$+ 450$$
_____

16. g
$$275$$
$$+ 155$$
_____

17. g
$$450$$
$$- 225$$
_____

18. g
$$600$$
$$- 375$$
_____

19. g
$$355$$
$$- 280$$
_____

20. g
$$540$$
$$- 175$$
_____

Assessment Test

1.   5924
   + 1798
   _____

2.   5007
   − 2148
   _____

3. £
     1·42
   + 3·88
   _____

4. Add three thousand six hundred and eighty-one, and four thousand and ninety-five.

5. Write five odd numbers under a hundred.

6. m
     6·74
   + 2·27
   _____

7.   g
     537
   − 188
   _____

8. m
     4·02
   − 2·75
   _____

9. Find the perimeter of this shape.

10.   127
    ×   8
    _____

11. 94 × 10

12. £
      1·49
    ×   4
    _____

13. Subtract 3247 from 6021.

14. Draw round a rectangle.
    Draw a line of symmetry.

15. Write the four points of the compass.

16. What fraction of the shape is coloured.

17. $4\overline{)228}$ 18. $6\overline{)138}$ 19. $3\overline{)225}$

20. Write this time.

21. Draw a graph to show this information.
    The vertical axis goes up in 2s.

Class	1	2	3	4	5	6
Number of children who stay for school lunch.	12	16	14	20	10	18

Glossary

a.m.　　　　before midday

compass

digit　　　　a single figure – for example, 6

even number　a number which can be divided exactly
　　　　　　　by 2

litre (l)　　a measure of liquid

millilitre (ml)　a measure of liquid

odd number　a number which cannot be divided
　　　　　　　exactly by 2

perimeter　　the distance round an object

p.m.　　　　after midday

right angle　a square corner

set square

symmetry　　this shape has a line of symmetry